HAVING A HAPPY MARRIAGE

How to prepare for a blissful marriage for singles and married

By

Hannah. G.M

DEDICATION

I dedicate this book to God Almighty.

TABLE OF CONTENT

CHAPTER ONE
INTRODUCTION

Marriage is a union between a man and a woman, the joining together of two opposites to form a whole or balance. Marriage is the coming together of two opposites to produce a whole or balance. Today, the term "marriage" refers to "the social institution under which a man and woman declare their choice to live as husband and wife by legal obligations, religious rituals."

It is generally known that men and women are distinct from one another, not just in their physical and physiological composition, but also in the way they see the world. Their respective motivations for tying

the knot in this day and age are distinct from one another. Women marry to secure their financial future, whereas males marry for sexual fulfillment.
The institution of marriage has evolved into a kind of commercial exchange between two parties. When one party perceives that the other is not looking out for their best interests, the "marriage" comes to an end and a divorce is finalized.

However, the "marriage" remains intact so long as the transaction is favorable to both sides. Intriguingly, those who lived during the period of the Vedas did not have the notion of divorce. The guy took entire responsibility for the woman's physical and financial requirements, and the woman cared for the man and his family with undivided affection and respect for the rest of their lives. The man accepted full responsibility for the woman's bodily and financial needs.

When it comes to a man's life, a woman is the "shakti." If a guy is compared to a car, then a woman is the gasoline that keeps the vehicle moving; without the fuel, the vehicle cannot move. Because of this, it is often believed that a woman who is fully devoted to a man can carry him to any height and that once he reaches that point, there is nothing in the physical world that he cannot do.

This is the kind of power that this marriage has. But things are so different than it used to be. Marriage in today's culture is more of a spectacular occasion than just the coming together of two individuals. The reasons range from the cultural pressure of marrying off the daughter to showing off one's riches to even simply being a feel-good factor!

The connection that is made between a man and a woman is contingent on their wants, and the duration of their relationship is directly proportional to those desires. The deeper the connection between us, the longer it will last.

Today, connections are typically made at the level of the mooladhar chakra, which only satisfies the baser needs of life, such as shelter, wealth, and belongings; there is no higher purpose; or at the level of the swadhishthan chakra, for sexual gratification. Neither of these connections serves any higher purpose. The manipoorak chakra is the location where connections for power and prestige are made. How often does one find themselves in a scenario in which they are so consumed with the need to be with a person that they cannot imagine that person being with anyone else, you want to know where and who they are with every second of the day, and you want to "possess" that person?

People sometimes confuse this sense of possessiveness and jealousy with the emotion known as "love." The surya chakra is the location where these connections are made, and love is not in any way responsible for their formation.

At the anahad chakra, a connection that is not motivated by self-interest is developed. In this connection, you love the other person but do not bind them down with conditions or emotions; rather, you let them free.

Even more uncommon are the connections that are made at the vishuddhi chakra when creativity is the driving force behind their establishment. The link that is made at the agya chakra, which is the seat of Lord Shiva inside a human being and is also the location where the union of Shiva and Shakti is finished, is the most subtle of all of the chakras.

But in the society we live in today, this is practically hard to do since most people are too preoccupied with attempting to fulfill their desires.

In times past, wedding rituals were simple and reverent, with the primary emphasis being on the joining of the bride and husband in wedlock and the subsequent harmony that followed. Everything from the food to the decorations to the ceremonies to the clothing and accessories was virtuous and had a purpose.

This is a very different world from the one we live in now. The list of events associated with weddings continues to get new additions on an annual basis. It seems as though there is no limit to the amount of money that may be thrown away or shown!

The ability of a modern man to spend money is directly proportionate to the degree to which he can celebrate and enjoy life. The fundamental purpose of the partnership is lost sight of as attention is paid to superficial aspects of the relationship. It is with great pleasure that international artists are recruited, a variety of international cuisines are offered, and it is required that loud music be played at all times... But what parent would even consider holding a Vedic havan in preparation for their child's wedding? Or providing food for the needy? Or just carrying out the responsibilities that come with being a parent without being so immersed in the role that they lose touch with the real world...

What could be beneficial about a connection between two people if the very act of their coming together turned out to be nothing more than a facade? It should come as no surprise that the phrase "happily ever after" in this day and age refers only to the conclusion of a fictional film. Let us return to our Vedic origins to bring back the sacredness of the marital institution.

Let us strive to be the force that brings peace and equilibrium into the world, rather than the source of its conflict and disharmony.

Some individuals have the desire to wed someone of a greater or lower social position than themselves. Others are interested in marrying somebody of similar social standing. In many civilizations, it is customary for women to wed men who have greater social rank than them. There are certain marriages in which both parties have sought out a mate with a status comparable to their own. There are further marriages in which the male is much older than the wife.

Some people are more interested in financial gain than in romantic commitment when it comes to romantic partnerships (thus a type of marriage of convenience). People who behave in this manner are sometimes referred to as gold diggers. Separate property systems, on the other hand, may be used to thwart the transfer of assets from one spouse to another in the case of death or divorce.

Men with higher incomes had a greater likelihood of getting married and a lower likelihood of being divorced. Women with higher incomes had a greater likelihood of being divorced.

In the tradition of English common law, from which modern legal doctrines and notions have grown, marriage was seen as a contract based upon a man and a woman making a private and voluntary agreement to become husband and wife.

This agreement formed the basis of marriage. It was widely believed that marriage served as the foundation of the family unit and was essential to the upkeep of morality and civilization.

Historically, it was the responsibility of the husband to provide a secure dwelling, make financial contributions toward the upkeep of the household, and occupy the same space as his wife. To fulfill her duties, the woman was required to take care of the household, reside in the same place as her husband, engage in sexual activity with him, and raise the couple's children. The fundamental idea that marriage is a legal contract is still there in modern times, but owing to developments in society, the legal responsibilities that come along with it have changed.

The states are primarily responsible for enforcing laws regarding marriage. The Supreme Court has decided that states have the authority to exercise reasonable control over the institution of marriage by dictating who is eligible for marriage and the procedures that may be used to end a marriage. The legal standing of both parties is altered at marriage, and this new status comes with a new set of rights and responsibilities for the husband and wife alike. However, one authority that the states do not have is the ability to ban marriage if there is not a good cause to do so.

CHAPTER TWO

DISCUSS BEFORE GOING IN

Some partners enter into their marriage with the mindset that it is the beginning of a journey during which they will get to know and love one other more deeply with each passing day. Others like having a more unobstructed view of the road they are going to travel before setting out on it.

To accomplish this aim, married couples should make an effort to discuss certain fundamental concerns that will likely arise in their lives together. These are some of the most crucial topics that should be discussed by those who are getting married soon.

1. Money and one's financial situation

The majority of divorces are brought on by monetary concerns. People who are getting ready to combine their households should talk about whether or not and how they will combine their finances. It is important to be transparent about both one's spending patterns and their current level of debt. It is mandatory to disclose any financial accounts.

Once it is discovered, having a hidden bank account is a surefire way to deal a significant blow to the relationship between the two people who are married. Couples need to talk about their finances and decide if they will combine their income from all sources, as well as their credit cards and bank accounts before they move in together.

Whether or not retirement accounts will be formed, how much each person may contribute monetarily toward the purchase of a house or automobile, and each person's perspective on saving, investing, and long-term financial objectives are other significant factors to consider.

The conversation should also be had regarding how one feels about lending money to family members, living within a predetermined monthly budget, and the appropriate level of debt to carry at any one time.

2. Property: When two people marry, both of them bring the property into the union. When seen from a legal perspective, the objects are regarded as belonging solely to the person in question. Partners need to talk about how they will approach future purchases. When it comes to dividing up property in the event of a divorce, for instance, the majority of jurisdictions consider a person's separate property any property acquired after marriage via means such as inheritance or gifts.

It is possible to avoid a disagreement in the future by beforehand determining how inheritance and any other assets that may be acquired from a parental estate will be handled. If one party or both bring the considerable property into the marriage, it is in everyone's best interest to discuss the possibility of entering into a prenuptial agreement.

3. Account of your past: It is asking for difficulties in the future to begin a marriage while keeping big secrets about your history hidden from your partner. Putting one's dirty laundry out in the open displays not just confidence in one's potential spouse but also a dedication to being truthful within the context of the relationship. It is in everyone's best interest to address concerns about family, health, previous alcohol or drug use, excessive gambling, or criminal activities right away.

4. Children and the role of a parent. You might be wondering how a couple who is about to get married could avoid discussing this issue, but in reality, the discussion is frequently replaced by assumption, and then the couple is surprised to discover that they have significant differences in views after they have been married for a few years. Before beginning a family, a couple needs to have a conversation about the number of children they foresee having and the particular conditions that should be met in each case.

How could being financially secure and making the right job choices influence the decision to have more children? Would it be possible to have a child via adoption in the case that health problems prevented pregnancy?

It is common for a person's parenting approach to be influenced by their background, and couples can bring quite diverse life experiences into a marriage. As a result, it makes perfect sense to investigate a few fundamental aspects of child-rearing. Will one of the parents decide to take on the role of a full-time stay-at-home parent after the baby is born? Will it be okay for both parents to utilize childcare while they are at work? Will there be a unified approach to punishment, or will it be carried out predominantly by one of the parents?

5. The spouse's family: In most cases, when two people marry, they both end up becoming members of the same newly enlarged family. This results in an overwhelming number of new connections to negotiate, as well as the possibility of new commitments.

Before getting married, a couple should talk about how much they anticipate interacting with their respective families following the wedding. Will your spouse's family anticipate your presence on specific holidays and special occasions? Will you celebrate occasions according to the customs that have been passed down in your family for generations, or will you create new customs along with your partner?

Will each family take turns to host the other on vacations? Think about the responsibilities that may come with helping to provide care for elderly parents.

6. Future residential plans: Choices in one's line of work could result in moving around quite a bit. It is important to have a conversation about where you and your spouse want to live once the decision is completely in your hands, and this is especially true if you and your partner were raised in different parts of the country. Do not assume that just because you spent your adolescence on the west coast, a partner who was raised in Florida would automatically be content to settle down thousands of miles away from their family just because you spent your upbringing on the west coast. Maintaining your adaptability while on site is a huge plus. Make sure that you are both operating from the same playbook.

7. **Personal time**: When two people get married, they each bring their circle of friends and a history of participating in leisure activities that they've found to be enjoyable. These may or may not be suitable with a new marriage depending on the individual. Couples should talk about how they feel about each other spending time apart with their friends or doing activities that they have grown to like on their own.

When one partner believes that everything should be enjoyed as a married pair, but the other partner wants to continue seeing his or her friends for things like a movie night, a game of golf, or a night out, resentment may rapidly build up between the two people.

In a similar vein, it is important to discuss how each individual feels about the other person seeing an ex-boyfriend or ex-girlfriend, as well as how each individual feels about the other person having a casual encounter with someone of the opposite gender for something like lunch or a drink after work. In most cases, it is unrealistic to anticipate that a partner would give up their long-standing relationships with friends and hobbies. Have a conversation about how you want to make the most of your time together and how much time you can reasonably expect to spend apart.

8. The resolving of conflicts: Arguments are inevitable. A newlywed couple may avoid having their union rapidly put in jeopardy by discovering how each partner handles dispute resolution. During a date, both parties should make an effort to behave their best.

Even while direct observation of conduct under pressure is likely to yield the most accurate response, couples should talk about how they handle stressful circumstances. Do you retreat yourself or do you get more physical? Are you easily angered and do you find that expressing your fury helps alleviate tension?

Talk about how you and your partner plan to manage extremely difficult situations, as well as how you will handle little concerns, such as having different tastes in home decor or leaving clothing strewn about the floor, and how you will resolve issues like these in the future.

9. Religion: Even while it can seem like a no-brainer to bring up this subject when dating, there are times when a more in-depth conversation is necessary. How significant a part does your faith play in your daily lives? How does the fact that you come from different religions impact your ability to parent a child? Will the fact that your partner does not share your religious views be a cause of contention in your relationship? What will happen if one spouse is a frequent churchgoer and the other does not attend services regularly?

10. Household duties: A discussion about who will be responsible for certain jobs around the home should usually take place. In some marriages, one partner may have grown up in a household in which weekly housekeepers took care of the household chores, whereas the other partner may have been raised in a family in which the parents expected their children to pitch in with the cooking and cleaning daily.

This can lead to friction in the relationship. When people have different standards for the order and cleanliness of their homes, it may rapidly develop tension that might have been easily avoided with a little bit of dialogue.

Every new dawn brings with it fresh opportunities for education. Even though you won't be able to anticipate all of the problems that might develop into arguments throughout your marriage, you should still be prepared to discuss the majority of the difficulties listed above at some time during your union. Instead of only wishing or assuming that your prospective husband is on the same page as your intentions, having some open and honest conversations can offer a solid basis on which to develop your relationship as you start your married life together.

CHAPTER THREE
KNOWING BASIC CONCEPTS

It goes without saying that the emotion of love alone is not enough to make a marriage effective; there are many other factors involved. To be able to care for and safeguard one another requires both a desire and the capacity to do so.

However, the presence of an enormous attraction between the two of you is the strongest indicator of whether or not you are capable of providing the necessary care and protection for one another.

If you and the other person are romantically involved, your partners are likely to see your relationship as a positive development for both of you and will refrain from interfering with its development. Your Givers are at liberty to present one another with the highest quality examples of what they each have to offer.

When two people are in love with one another, they are better able to fulfill the emotional requirements of the other. They make you more loving, sexual, talkative, recreational, honest, and admiring, which are all impulses you may not have realized you had before. When one is in love, all of these things seem to happen rather effortlessly.

When you are no longer in love with each other, though, anything that will assist your marriage appears artificial. Your natural inclination is to move away from trying to save your marriage and toward ending it.

To assist you to do what it takes to restore your love for each other when you are not in love with each other and when you do not feel like doing any of the things that are necessary to do so, I have developed these Basic Concepts. Then, after your love has been repaired, these ideas will assist you in maintaining it for the remainder of your life together as a couple.

If you take all of these tips and apply them to your marriage, you will accomplish something that the vast majority of married couples strive for but are unable to achieve: falling in love and remaining in love. And eventually, this is what will rescue a marriage: rekindling the sense of love between the two partners. These concepts include the following:

1. THE LOVE BANK

In the course of my efforts to understand how to rescue marriages, I ultimately realized that the most effective approach to do so was to instruct couples on how to first fall in love with one another and then continue to feel that love for one another.

As a result, I devised a concept that I dubbed the Love Bank to assist couples in comprehending the factors that cause individuals to fall in and out of love. This idea, probably more than any other that I conceived, assisted couples in understanding that almost everything they did had an effect, either good or bad, on the love that they felt for one another. And with that insight, the majority of them embarked on a path of action that not only kept their love alive but also kept their marriages intact.

The method in which each individual interacts with us is recorded in the Love Bank that is inside each one of us. Everyone we know has an account, and the various things they do either add to or take away from the love units that are stored in their accounts.

It is your feelings' way of urging you to spend time with the people who bring out the best in you. When you think of someone fondly, you deposit into the "Love Bank" account that corresponds to that person. And the sensation of love is triggered if the Love Bank reaches a particular amount of deposits (the romantic love threshold).

As long as your Love Bank balance is greater than that threshold, you will continue to feel love for as long as the threshold is met. But as soon as it dips below that level, you will no longer have that sensation. You will have feelings of like for anybody whose balance is more than zero, but you can only fall in love with someone whose balance is greater than the love threshold.

However, your feelings do more than just urge you to spend time with people who bring you joy; they also discourage you from spending time with those who bring you sadness. Every time you think of someone in a negative light, you take money out of your "Love Bank." In addition, the value of your Love Bank account might become negative if you take out more money than you put in.

When anything like this occurs, Love Bank is converted into Hate Bank.
Those with negative balances that are somewhat over the threshold for dislike may irritate you, but those with balances that are far below the threshold for dislike will make you despise the individual.

Try going through life with a partner whom you despise! Your feelings are exerting every effort to get you out of this situation, and filing for divorce is one of the most reasonable options available to you at this point.

My services are often sought out by married couples who are on the verge of giving up on their relationship. Their Love Banks have been suffering losses of love units for such a significant amount of time that they are now significantly in the red.

And the fact that they have negative balances in their Love Banks makes it difficult for them to even be in the same room together without feeling awkward. They cannot even fathom making it through another year of marriage, much alone the possibility of ever falling in love again.

However, it is my responsibility to assist them in rediscovering the love they formerly had for one another. I strongly suggest that they cease taking money out of their Love Bank account and instead begin adding money to their account. To assist couples in accomplishing those goals, I conceived of and developed all of the additional Basic Concepts.

2. HABITS AND INSTINCTS IN HUMAN BEHAVIOR

Habits are ingrained behavioral patterns that we have developed through time, while instincts are natural tendencies that we are born with. Both of them have a propensity to repeat themselves over and over again in an almost effortless manner.

They are crucial in our discussion of what it takes to be in love since our conduct is what creates deposits and withdrawals from Love Banks, and our instincts and habits make up the majority of our behavior. Therefore, we must take into account these things.

Love Bank deposits may be made by instincts and habits; thus, it is vital to know how to establish such habits, since once they are acquired, deposits can be made frequently and almost easily. This is why it is so important to know how to create those habits.

Unfortunately, many of our inclinations and behaviors, such as lashing out in anger, contribute to the process of taking money out of our Love Bank account. They are so common that they play a very significant part in the eradication of Love Bank accounts because they are repeated so often. If we want to put an end to people taking money out of the Love Bank, we need to find a way to put an end to harmful inclinations and behaviors. Although it is more difficult to break habits than instincts, it is possible to live without either.

As we go through the remaining ideas, it is important to bear in mind both the benefits of developing positive habits and the drawbacks of developing negative habits. This is because the influence that these behaviors have on Love Bank balances is compounded when they are repeated.

3. THE PRIMARY AND PRIMARILY IMPORTANT EMOTIONAL REQUIREMENTS

What is the most efficient method for transferring love units into one another's love banks? When I initially started exploring how to preserve marriages, I conducted interviews with what seemed like hundreds of different couples to discover the answer to this issue. After some time, I was able to piece together their response: you have to accommodate the most significant emotional requirements of one another.

You and your partner fell in love with one another because you brought a great deal of joy to one another's lives, and the reason why you brought such joy to one another was because you satisfied a number of significant emotional requirements that each of you had. The only way for you and your partner to maintain the love you have is to continue addressing each other's needs. It is possible for the emotion of love to return, even after it has been absent for an extended period or after it has completely vanished. It is possible to get it back if the two of you resume making significant contributions to the Love Bank.

4 . THE STRATEGY OF UNSPLITTING ONE'S ATTENTION

If you and your partner do not make a weekly appointment to give each other your whole attention, it will be hard for you to fulfill the most significant emotional requirements of one another. As a result, I have written the Policy of Undivided Attention to assist you and your partner in creating time in your respective schedules for one another.

Each week, you should be sure to give your partner at least fifteen hours of your full attention.

Make the most of this opportunity to satisfy your emotional need for love, discussion, leisure, friendship, and sexual gratification.
By following this strategy, you will be able to steer clear of one of the most typical blunders that couples do throughout their marriage: ignoring one another.

But this goes beyond only making it more likely that you will satisfy the emotional requirements of one another. It is also the key that opens the door to the application of all the other fundamental ideas.
You will not be able to avoid Love Busters and you will not be able to bargain successfully if you do not have enough time to give each issue your full and undivided attention. Time spent giving one another one's complete and undivided attention is

an essential component of everything that makes a marriage successful.

Despite this, the majority of married couples, particularly after the birth of children, choose to substitute their time spent together with activities that are of lower priority. You most likely engaged in the same behavior. You both made an effort to fulfill each other's requirements with the available time, but unfortunately, there wasn't much time available. Your inability to spend quality time together in private may have been a major contributor to your misery, but you believed you had no choice but to accept it. It's also possible that you've found yourself suppressing the genuine expression of your emotions since there just wasn't an acceptable moment to speak about them.

If you make spending time alone with each other your top priority, you may ensure that it will never be supplanted by other activities that have a lower significance. Your job, the time you spend with your kids, the upkeep of your house, and a whole host of other obligations will all fight for the little amount of time you have together. However, if you adhere to the Principle of Undivided Attention, you will not let anything take away from the time that you spend together since it is so valuable and important.

When you and your partner want to offer each other your whole attention (you want solitude), it is necessary for you to spend some time apart from your children and your other pals.

When you are together, make the most of the time to satisfy the emotional demands of love, discussion, recreational companionship, and sexual pleasure (since when these needs are satisfied, the biggest deposit in the Love Bank is made!);

Set aside a minimum of fifteen hours in each week to spend time together, since this is the typical amount of time required to fulfill the four requirements. You gave each other this level of care while you were dating, and it helped you fall in love with one another. People who have affairs continue to show each other this type of care to maintain their feelings of love for the partner with whom they are having the affair.

Why should the only periods that lead to love being generated be during courting and affairs? Why is it that it can't also happen in married life? It is possible if you commit to devoting a certain amount of time to one another weekly in the form of undivided attention.

5. LOVE BUSTERS

When two people can fulfill the most significant emotional needs of one another, they transform into each other's primary source of pleasure. However, if you are not cautious, the two of you have the potential to become each other's biggest cause of sadness.

It is a waste of time to deposit love units if you are just going to withdraw them immediately away. Therefore, in addition to taking care of your significant emotional needs, you should also make it a priority to keep your partner and the Love Bank safe from harm.

This may be accomplished by paying attention to how your ordinary behaviors might make each other miserable.

Both you and your partner were born with the personality traits of being demanding, disrespectful, furious, obnoxious, independent, and dishonest. These are natural human characteristics, but I refer to them as "Love Busters" since they undermine the sense of love that partners have for one another.

If, however, you make a pact with your partner that you will never be the reason for their sadness, then you will do whatever it takes to rid yourself of these harmful habits to save your relationship with your partner. You will not only be safeguarding your partner by ridding your home of Love Busters, but you will also be maintaining your partner's love for you in the process.

6. RADICAL HONESTY AS A POLICY

Honesty should take precedence over anything else in your relationship with your partner if you want the two of you to feel romantically attracted to one another. The reason for this is because it plays such a significant part in the development of romantic love.

It is one of the ten most essential emotional wants, and having it satisfied may lead to the experience of experiencing love for another person. On the other hand, its antithesis, dishonesty, is a Love Buster since it brings to the end of romantic relationships.

However, there is a second reason why honesty is so important in the process of developing love: honesty is the only way that you and your partner can ever begin to understand one another. Without honesty, it is impossible to make the modifications that are necessary to both make each other happy and keep from making each other unhappy.

Being truthful is not a simple task. Honesty is a virtue that is not widely held in today's society, and the majority of couples have not committed to being honest with one

another. There is a school of thought held by a good number of marital counselors and clergymen that asserts honesty is not always the best approach.
They believe that it is both harsh and selfish to reveal one's previous transgressions, as well as to make such disclosures. Even while it may help you feel better to get something off your chest, doing so may cause your spouse to experience discomfort. They contend that the most compassionate action one can do is to cover up their faults or, at the very least, to put them out of sight.

And if it is compassionate to lie about sins that have been committed in the past, then why is it not compassionate to lie about sins that have been committed in the present or that will be committed in the future?

In my opinion, this is the same as allowing the proverbial camel's nose inside the tent. At some point, you will sit down to dinner with the camel. Either being honest is always the best course of action, or you'll always find a reason to justify being dishonest.

7. THE RECIPIENT AND THE DONATOR

Have you ever considered the possibility that your partner is influenced by an evil spirit? You'll find yourself dealing with self-centeredness and lack of consideration one minute, then the next, the person will be kind and caring toward you. Believe me when I say that the adversary you face is not a demon but rather the contrasting aspects of our character. I refer to the two of them as the Giver and the Taker.

We are all motivated by the desire to improve the lives of those around us. We hope that other people will be happy, and we want to do everything we can to help make that happen. When we have such thoughts, it is a sign that our Giver is affecting us.

The golden rule of a Giver is to do anything you can to make other people happy and to steer clear of anything that causes the distress of others, even if it causes you distress as well. It inspires us to use that guideline in the ways that we interact with other people in our lives.

Taking affects everyone, but at the same time, we desire what's best for ourselves. Along with you, we wish to enjoy life. When we have felt like that, it is because our Taker is affecting us. Rule number one for a Taker is to do anything you can to make yourself happy, and to avoid doing anything that makes you miserable, even if it causes others to be upset as a result. If you ever find that this rule makes sense to you, then know that it is because your Taker is in command.

When we interact with other people, these two fundamental facets of our personality often coexist in a state of equilibrium. However, it is common for married couples to take turns becoming the head of the household.

And this is the root cause of the majority of the issues that married couples face. If we follow the advice of our Giver, we are ready to suffer to make our spouse happy. If, on the other hand, we follow the advice of our Taker, we are prepared to let our spouse suffer for us to be happy, then we are willing to suffer ourselves. In either scenario, the guidance we are given is not well thought out since it always results in someone being injured.

8. THE THREE ATTITUDES THAT ARE REQUIRED IN A MARRIAGE

The Giver and the Taker are responsible for the emotions that I refer to as states of mind. These mental states have a significant impact on the strategies that a husband and wife use to overcome disagreements that arise in their relationship.

However, in each of these three states of mind, it is very hard to negotiate. This is one of the factors that makes bargaining in marriage, in general, so challenging.

The state of intimacy is where we often find ourselves when we are feeling content and in love. This frame of mind is managed by the Giver, and as a result, we are encouraged to adhere to the Giver's rule, which states that you should do everything in your power to ensure the happiness of your partner, and you should steer clear of anything that could potentially upset them, even if it would also make you unhappy.

Because we are not bargaining with our interests in mind, following that rule might lead to the development of routines that may be beneficial for our partner but may have catastrophic consequences for us.

Regrettably, faulty agreements reached in the state of Intimacy have the potential to bring about our sadness, which in turn rouses the sleeping Taker. When we begin experiencing feelings of unhappiness, our Taker rushes to our aid and sets in motion the events that lead to a state of conflict. As long as we are content, our Taker has nothing to do. We are urged to follow the rule that you should do anything you can to make yourself happy, and you should avoid anything that makes you sad, even if it causes other people to be unhappy. This rule applies even if the Taker is now in control.

In addition, The Taker pushes us to be demanding, rude, and furious in the direction of our spouses in an attempt to coerce them into making us happy. The Taker's preferred method of conducting negotiations is to fight.

When battling doesn't work and we are still dissatisfied, the Taker pushes us to choose a different path of action that results in the State of Withdrawal. This happens when we are still unhappy. Our Taker wants us to completely give up on our spouse rather than attempting to coerce them into making us happy by whatever means necessary. We don't want our partners to do anything for us, and we don't want to do anything for them either. Neither of us wants to help the other. When we are in this frame of mind, we are emotionally estranged from one another.

Once a couple realizes that they are stuck in the state of withdrawal, what steps can they take to begin working their way back to the state of intimacy? And after they have returned, how are they going to continue living there?

9. THE PRACTICE OF COMMON CONSENT AS A POLICY

The impulses of a married couple are not conducive to fair discussion. They either result in stealing a bank (State of Intimacy) or handing away the shop (State of Intimacy) (State of Conflict). When someone is in the state of withdrawal, they do not even have the desire to negotiate.

However, spouses need to negotiate fairly to satisfy each other's most significant requirements and stay away from things that might be detrimental to their love for one another over time.

You need a rule to assist you to overcome the counsel of your Giver and Taker, which tends to be focused on the here and now. Their advice lacks foresight since it doesn't matter what the regulation is, someone will always be wounded.

When we follow the advice of the Taker, it causes harm to our partner, but when we follow the advice of the Giver, it causes harm to ourselves. As a result, I came up with a guideline to ensure that nobody gets wounded, which should be the end aim of any discussion that is considered fair. This regulation will henceforth be referred to as the Policy of Joint Agreement.

Never embark on a project of any kind without first obtaining your partner's wholehearted approval.
Almost everything you do has some kind of influence on something else. Therefore, it is extremely crucial to be aware of what the result of that action will be before you carry it out. You will be reminded to confer with one another thanks to the Policy of Joint Agreement, which will ensure that you do not end up being the unhappy party in the relationship of the other.

In addition to this, it makes the necessity of negotiation present at all times, regardless of your state of mind. If you both agree to this policy, then you will not be able to do anything without the enthusiastic agreement of the other person. Because of this, it will be necessary for the two of you to discuss your plans and negotiate while keeping the feelings of the other person in mind. You are going to have a very difficult time reaching a satisfying agreement if the negotiation process is not calm and pleasant.

However, there are several exemptions to these rules and regulations. It is not something that should be followed if it puts the health or safety of either partner in jeopardy. For instance, if one spouse in a marriage commits physical abuse against the other, the injured spouse needs to report it to the authorities even if the abuser's partner is opposed to this course of action. Exposing adultery is another example of an exception that should be made since a betrayed spouse's mental health is put in jeopardy if they keep the affair a secret from themselves. Some partners make an effort to take advantage of this policy to prevent their partners from having any kind of regular interaction with the outside world.

Both partners in a marriage must have access to a secure and positive living environment. Therefore, you should not adhere to this policy if you believe that doing so might put your well-being or the well-being of others in jeopardy.

The Policy of Radical Honesty and the Policy of Joint Agreement work together to assist you in the process of developing an open and integrated way of life, the kind of lifestyle that will ensure your love for one another. They also prevent the establishment of a hidden second life, which is crucial since adultery is the most dangerous risk to a marriage and may flourish in a dark, damp place like a basement.

10. GUIDELINES FOR SUCCESSFUL NEGOTIATION

If you and your partner are arguing over anything, my advice is for you to refrain from taking any action until you and your partner have concluded that you both feel passionate about. However, what steps should you take to ensure that this agreement is reached? I propose you follow four fundamental principles.

The first piece of advice is to agree upon certain ground rules that will make the discussion more comfortable and secure.

- Rule No. 1: Attempt to have a friendly and upbeat demeanor during the discussions.
- Rule number two: Put your own safety first. During the course of the negotiation, you should avoid making demands, displaying disrespect, or becoming upset, regardless of whether or not your spouse engages in any of these behaviors toward you.
- Rule number three: If the two of you have reached a stalemate and do not seem to be making any progress, or if one of you is beginning to make

demands, show disrespect, or grow upset, you must cease negotiating and return to the problem at a later time.

The second principle is to identify the issue from both points of view while showing mutual respect for those points of view.

The next piece of advice is to engage in unrestrained brainstorming so that you may give your imagination a chance to find answers that will make you and your partner pleased. Bring a notepad and a pencil with you wherever you go so that you may scribble down ideas as soon as they come to you during the day.

- Guideline 4 Select the answer that most completely satisfies the requirements of the Policy of Joint Agreement, which include having both parties' enthusiastic agreement. When there is a disagreement, you should always bear in mind how important it is to find a solution that will put as many love units as possible into the relationship while preventing any withdrawals. Also, be sure that the method you choose to locate this answer not only prevents withdrawals but also deposits love units.

CHAPTER FOUR
THE SUCCESS PRINCIPLES

Intelligent partners are essential to a healthy marriage. They educate themselves by perusing articles on the Internet, reading books, going to seminars, and seeing other happy couples. On the other hand, happy couples will tell you that they have also learned a lot via experience and by making mistakes.

The following is a list of the top ten success principles that I have discovered through working with and seeing hundreds of different couples:

1 Being happy is not the most essential thing in the world. Everyone has the goal of achieving happiness, but the reality is that pleasure is fleeting. When life takes away their happiness, successful couples have learned to consciously engage in activities that would help them regain it.

2. A couple that has established a strong marriage realizes the importance of just being there. When things are difficult for a couple and they are at a loss for what to do, they need to stick together and be there for their partner. The passage of time has a way of assisting couples in working through their issues by presenting them with chances to de-stress and triumph over obstacles.

3. You may expect the same consequence if you continue to behave in the same manner as before. Wise couples have learned that to receive various outcomes from a situation, they need to approach it differently. The success or failure of a marriage may often be determined by seemingly little changes in approach, attitude, and behavior.

4. Your attitude does matter. Altering one's mentality is just as vital as modifying one's actions in this regard. A negative attitude is typically the root cause of negative emotions and behaviors.

5. If you change your opinion, you should probably also alter your marriage. How a couple thinks about their partner and what they believe about that person both have an impact on how each of them sees the other. It is very important both what they expect from their partner and how they treat them.

6. The areas of your lawn that get the most water have the greenest grass. The notion that "the grass is greener" — that is, the idea that "someone else would make me happy" — is one that spouses in good marriages have learned to combat. They have realized the importance of focusing their efforts on strengthening both themselves and their marriage.

7. If you want to make changes in your marriage, start with yourself. Couples who have been together for a long time have realized that attempting to alter the behavior of their partner is similar to pulling on a rope; it is almost impossible. Frequently, the only person in our marriages who we can alter is ourselves.

8. Love is not simply an emotion; it is also a verb. The "feel-good aspect of marriage" is eventually worn away by the day-to-day grind of married life. Feelings, like happiness, are subject to change; yet, true love is founded on the vows of commitment made by a couple to one another: "For better or for worse" — both when it feels good and when it doesn't feel good.

9. The struggle that frequently takes place inside a marriage must be fought between the ears. The partners in a healthy marriage have developed the ability to put aside personal grievances and avoid dwelling on the relationship's history. They are aware of the fact that not only did they marry a flawed person, but so did their partner.

10. Just because there is a problem does not imply that the marriage is ended. Crises are similar to hurricanes in that they are terrifying, disruptive, and hazardous. But you have to keep driving if you want to make it through the storm. An emergency offers an opportunity for a fresh start. Great individuals and happy relationships are often the product of enduring hardship together.

Being married requires you to sacrifice a part of who you are. You can't ignore the other person if you want to go somewhere. And that's usually where things go wrong in a marriage. We often place a higher priority on our thoughts and the maintenance of our health. The culture in which we are raised also influences the way we think and act.

How do we look at our partner? Do you consider him or her to be on the same level as you? Whether we are aware of it or not, most of the time we don't give our partner's emotions and requirements the full consideration they need. Maybe neither of your parents taught you how to do it correctly, or maybe you were forced to grow up without one or both of your parents for a period when you were young.

On top of that, males and women have fundamentally distinct mental processes. Women and men experience their emotions differently and as a result, respond differently to similar circumstances. This may result in several misunderstandings inside the marriage.

CHAPTER FIVE
UNDERSTANDING CONFLICT RESOLUTION

It all begins with each one of us. The vast majority of the time, our thoughts begin with ourselves. Even when you are being really helpful, you may be doing it because you believe it is required of you or because it gives you a positive feeling.

If one of you puts your own needs ahead of those of the other, your relationship will deteriorate. One of you may be preoccupied with the advancement of his or her work or the care of the children. There is insufficient attention that can be given to the relationship. Or, one of the two decides that they would be happier with someone else and cheats on you with another person.

If you offer your spouse insufficient amounts of attention and respect, that person will react by, for example, withdrawing emotionally, becoming angry, or attempting to restore equilibrium via some other means. Before you realize it, you will have suffered serious emotional scars that are difficult to recover from. The longer these issues continue to exist, the more those wounds will get infected.

It's also possible that one of the partners is keeping anything from the other that they shouldn't be. For instance, a dependency, certain expenditures, or other challenges. Even though you may believe that the other person is unaffected by it, the truth is that it will always have an impact on the relationship.

The 6 Steps to Successfully Resolve Conflict in Your Marriage

Even though few partners prefer to acknowledge it, the argument is an inevitable part of any marriage. We have had our fair share of disputes, and some of how we have disagreed with one another have not been nice. We could easily fill an entire book with examples of bad behavior!

Begin with two self-centered persons who come from various backgrounds and have distinctive personalities. Then come to the negative routines, the fascinating quirks, the expectations, and finally the day-to-day challenges that life throws at you to crank up the heat a little bit. What do you think? You can't avoid having arguments all the time. It's unavoidable.

It is not possible to prevent difficulties in a marriage since every marriage has them; what matters is how you choose to respond to them when they arise. The resolution of a conflict may be a unifying or isolating experience for everyone involved. You and your partner need to decide on how you will behave in times of dispute.

The first step in resolving a problem is to recognize, acknowledge, and make peace with the differences between you and the other party.

Since of this, there is often tension in our marriage because our personalities are so different. People who are more focused on their work tend to marry those who are more concerned with their relationships. People who go through life at a breakneck speed sometimes find themselves paired with partners who have a more sedate approach to life. It's weird, but I guess that's part of the explanation for why you married the person you did. Your life did not previously have the variety, spice, or distinctiveness that it has now because of the addition of your spouse.

But after being married for some time (often just a short period), the things that attracted them become those that turn them off. You and your partner can get into an argument about anything as trivial as how to correctly squeeze a bottle of toothpaste or as significant as your divergent philosophies on how to handle finances or raise children. You may discover that your histories and your personalities are so unlike to one another, leaving you to question how and why God brought the two of you together in the first place.

It is essential to have an awareness of these distinctions, after which one must learn to accept and accommodate them. You are obligated to accept God's gift to you, just as Adam did when he received Eve as a gift from God. God provided you with a partner who, in ways that you haven't even figured out yet, complements you perfectly and makes you whole.

The second step is to recognize that overcoming selfishness is necessary to successfully resolve conflicts.

When we get married, every one of our idiosyncrasies is amplified because it gives fuel to what is unquestionably the most significant cause of our friction: our fallen and self-centered nature.

Since Adam and Eve, marriage has been fraught with difficulty in terms of maintaining peace. It is impossible for a couple that starts their marriage together intending to live their own self-centered, separate lives to ever have any chance of experiencing the oneness that God intended for marriage. The issue was correctly expressed by the prophet Isaiah more than

2,500 years ago when he defined the fundamental egotism of humans in the following manner: "All of us like sheep have gone astray, each of us has turned to his path" (Isaiah 53:6). We are all preoccupied with ourselves; we all have a natural tendency to watch out for number one, which inevitably results in contention.

The institution of marriage presents a fantastic opportunity to address the problem of selfishness. The strategy outlined in the Bible has already been successful in our lives, and it continues to do so daily. God is the one who has transformed us, not each other.

He is the one who has changed us. Jesus and his teachings provide the solution to the problem of selfishness in the world. He demonstrated to us that we need to be content with coming in last rather than aspiring to be first. Instead of asking to be served, we need to be the ones doing the serving. We must sacrifice our lives rather than work to save them.

We are obligated to love our immediate community, which consists of our partners, as much as we love ourselves. In a nutshell, if we want to triumph against selfishness, we have to surrender, give in, and offer all we have.

Step Three: To resolve a problem, it is necessary to pursue the other person.

Romans 12:18 instructs believers to "live peaceably with all men" if it is feasible and as much as it relies on them to do so. The more I live, the more I can appreciate how challenging those words may be for a lot of different couples. To live peacefully implies to actively seek peace. It involves not waiting for the other person to take the first move toward resolving a tough disagreement but rather taking the initiative to do it yourself.

Putting aside your pain, anger, and resentment to work toward resolving a problem requires you to be emotionally detached. It signifies keeping one's hope alive. The phrase "keep your connections current" is a challenge that I issue to you.

To put it another way, make it a point to commit to maintaining a strong fellowship with your spouse daily, as well as with your children, parents, colleagues, and friends. Do not allow Satan to win by separating you from a person whose well-being you care about.

In the fourth step, you will learn that conflict resolution involves loving confrontation.

Wordsworth once remarked that a person who has a trustworthy friend does not need a vanity mirror. When both partners in a marriage believe that their partner is a wonderful friend who will listen, understand, and help them work through any difficulty or disagreement, such marriage may be considered blessed. To achieve this successfully, loving confrontation is required.

It takes prudence, patience, and humility to confront your partner with grace and tactfulness. Additional helpful hints that we've uncovered include the following:

Examine the driving force behind you. Are you going to help or harm with your words? Will discussing this issue lead to healing, completeness, and oneness, or will it lead to greater isolation?

Examine your frame of mind. Confrontation with love conveys the message, "I care about you. I have respect for you, and I expect the same in return. I am interested in how you are feeling. You shouldn't go on your bulldozer and try to take out your husband. Take a compassionate approach toward your partner.
Investigate the context carefully. This covers the time as well as the place and the scene.

It is best to avoid having a confrontation with your partner at inopportune times, such as when he is exhausted after a long day's work or while he is mediating a dispute between the kids. Also, you should never mock, make fun of, or dispute with your partner in front of other people.

Investigate the possibility of the presence of additional pressures. Be understanding of the perspective that your partner is coming from. Where does your spouse's life currently stand in the grand scheme of things?

Listen to your spouse. Make an effort to comprehend his or her position, and ask questions to elucidate points of view.

Be sure that you are not just capable of dishing it out, but also of taking it. You may start giving your partner some "kind counsel," but you'll quickly realize that what you're referring to is not his issue, but rather yours.

Maintain focus on a single topic at a time during the conversation. Do not bring up a number of them. It's not fair to your partner to have them listen to all of your gripes at once, so don't let them build up.

Put less emphasis on the individual and more on the issue at hand. For instance, you need a budget, but your partner has a reputation for being a bit of a spendthrift. Work through the financial plans and make the absence of a budget the adversary, rather than your partner in the relationship.

Pay more attention to how you behave than to who you are. Another time, the "you" message will be contrasted with the "I" message.

You may destroy the reputation of your partner and pierce his or her heart by sending "you" messages to him or her, such as "You're always late—you don't care about me at all; you don't care about anybody except yourself." The message that starts with "I" might say something like, "I get annoyed when you don't let me know that you'll be late.

I would be grateful if you could give me a call so that we may discuss other potential options."

Instead of passing judgment on people's intentions, concentrate on the facts. If your partner forgets to make an essential call, rather than saying something like, "You're so irresponsible; you only do things to upset me," it is better to deal with the repercussions of what you both have to do next.

Above all else, prioritize knowing your partner above determining who is winning or losing the argument. When confronted by your partner, pay close attention not just to what is said but also to what is not said. For instance, he may be furious about something that occurred at work, and the fact that he's taking out his frustration on you means that you're bearing the brunt of the burden.

Fifth Step: Forgiveness is necessary to end a quarrel.

It doesn't matter how much effort two people put into loving and appeasing one another; they won't be successful. When you fail, you damage yourself. The healing balm of forgiveness is the only thing that can ease the ache that one feels.

Asking for and granting forgiveness promptly is essential to preserving an open, personal, and joyful atmosphere inside a marriage. And the capacity to accomplish that is directly related to the connection that each person has with God.

Jesus had this to say about the act of forgiving others: "For if you forgive others for their trespasses, your heavenly Father will also forgive you for your faults." But if you do not forgive men, neither will your Father forgive the offenses that you have committed (Matthew 6:14–15). The command is unmistakable: God requires us to forgive one another, and marriage, arguably more than any other relationship, provides numerous opportunities to put this teaching into practice.

To forgive someone requires letting go of the anger and the need to exact revenge. You have absolved the other person of responsibility via a deliberate act of your own will. And as a Christian, you do not submit to this while kicking and screaming in protest while being forced to do so. Instead, you should approach it with a spirit of gentleness and love, as the apostle, Paul urged: "show kindness to one another, forgive each other just like our Lord Jesus Christ has forgiven you.

Sixth Step: To resolve a quarrel, it is necessary to return a blessing for an insult.

In First Peter chapter three verses 8 and 9, it is written, "To summarize, all of you be harmonious, sympathetic, brotherly, kindhearted, and humble in spirit; do not pay evil for evil, but do good in place of evil; for you were assigned this very mission, so you may inherit your blessings."

Every marriage functions based on either an "insult for insult" or a "blessing for insult" connection between the couple. It's not uncommon for husbands and wives to become quite skilled at hurling insults at one another, whether it be about the way he looks, the way she cooks, the way he drives, or the way she cleans the home. It seems that many married couples have no idea how else to interact with one another.

What does it mean to give someone the benefit of the doubt after they have insulted you? The following is found in the third chapter of 1 Peter and it says, "For, 'the one who wishes life, to love and see happy days, must guard his mouth against evil and his lips from saying deception." He has to stop doing evil and start doing good; he needs to look for peace and work toward it.'" (verses 10-11).

To put others before yourself and offer a blessing first requires you to stand aside or just refuse to take revenge if your partner becomes furious. Altering your natural propensity to lash out, fight back, or tell your spouse off is just about as simple as changing the course of the Mississippi River. Change your natural tendency to tell your husband off. Without the assistance of God and without submitting to the guidance of the Holy Spirit, you can't succeed.

It also signifies acting positively. There are times when doing good requires nothing more than a few words said softly and kindly, or maybe a touch, such as a hug or a pat on the shoulder. It might involve going out of your way to do something kind for your partner as part of a concerted attempt to win their approval.

In conclusion, being a gift requires actively searching for and achieving a state of calm. You are not seeking solitude when you actively want forgiveness; rather, you are on the path to oneness.

Even though it might be challenging, we can claim God's promises when we are working through marital difficulties. Not only does God praise our efforts when they are founded on His Word, but He also reveals to us that He has an ultimate purpose for the difficulties we face. The trials we face are meant to put our faith to the test, cultivate perseverance in us, help us become more refined, and ultimately bring glory to God. This is the optimism that He instills in us: that we may truly see our disagreements as a chance to grow in our faith and bring glory to God.

www.ingramcontent.com/pod-product-compliance
Lightning Source LLC
LaVergne TN
LVHW052045160826
845678LV00015B/3118